W9-CDM-952

COVID-19

The Science of the Coronavirus

by Renae Gilles

LERNER PUBLICATIONS ◆ MINNEAPOLIS

Lerner Publications Company
An imprint of Lerner Publishing Group, Inc.
241 First Avenue North
Minneapolis, MN 55401 USA

For reading levels and more information, look up this title at www.lernerbooks.com.

All facts and data represented in this book were accurate according to sources available as of May 2020.

Image credits: Zimniy/Shutterstock, p. 1; DKosig/Getty Images, p. 3 (top); Jamie Grill/Blend Images/Getty Images, p. 3 (bottom left); photoguns/Getty Images, p. 3 (middle); Couleur/Pixabay, p. 3 (bottom right); Radoslav Zilinsky/Getty Images, p. 5; Design Cells/Getty Images, p. 6; Jamie Grill/Blend Images/Getty Images, p. 7 (bottom); Thomas Tolstrup/Getty Images, p. 7 (top); filadendron/Getty Images, p. 8; jamielawton/Getty Images, p. 9; Nitat Termmee/Getty Images, p. 11; Stringer/Getty Images, p. 12; Marco Di Lauro/Getty Images, p. 13 (left); Basile Morin/Wikimedia, p. 13 (right); skynesher/Getty Images, p. 14; David Dee Delgado/Getty Images, p. 15 (right); Marco Di Lauro/Getty Images, p. 15 (left); Carol Yepes/Getty Images, p. 17; xia yuan/Getty Images, p. 18; Quinn Dombrowski/Flickr, p. 19 (top); Teeramet Thanomkiat/EyeEm/Getty Images, p. 19 (bottom); eamesBot/Shutterstock, p. 20; AfricaImages/Getty Images, p. 21; Pordee_Aomboon/Shutterstock, p. 23; Bill Oxford/Getty Images, p. 24; Jose A. Bernat Bacete/Getty Images, p. 25 (bottom); SDI Productions/Getty Images, p. 25 (top); Halfpoint/Shutterstock, p. 26; RUSSELLTATEdotCOM/Getty Images, p. 27 (bottom); sabelskaya/Getty Images, p. 27 (middle); Olga W Boeva/Shutterstock, p. 27 (top); DKosig/Getty Images, p. 28 (top); photoguns/Getty Images, p. 28 (middle); Couleur/Pixabay, p. 28 (bottom); lineartestpilot/Shutterstock, p. 29; Background: gaisonok/Getty Images; Cover: Paul Biris/Getty Images (bottom); Zimniy/Shutterstock (top); Fact icon: sinisamaric1/Pixabay

Main body text set in Minion Pro.
Typeface provided by Adobe Originals.

Editor: Lauren Dupuis-Perez **Designer**: Deron Payne

Library of Congress Cataloging-in-Publication Data
The Cataloging-in-Publication Data for *COVID-19: The Science of the Coronavirus* is on file at the Library of Congress.
ISBN 978-1-72842-800-0 (lib. bdg.)

Manufactured in the United States of America
Corporate Graphics, North Mankato, MN

CONTENTS

A New Virus

In 2019, a new sickness emerged. Hundreds of people were suddenly falling ill. Doctors and health officials were alarmed. Scientists raced to study the sickness. They discovered it was caused by a tiny germ. They named the **virus** SARS-CoV-2.

This **novel** virus swept across the world. The virus causes a disease called COVID-19. Millions of people got sick. Hospitals began filling up. People took action. They wanted to slow the virus's spread. Politicians worked with health experts. They made new rules. Students stopped going to school. Business owners closed their shops. People stayed home from work. Many people lost their jobs.

Within months, the entire world was different. Over 7 billion lives were changed forever. And it all started with one little speck of SARS-CoV-2.

DID YOU KNOW?

SARS-CoV-2 is extremely small. It is 120 nanometers across. Your fingernails grow 1 nanometer every second.

virus: a tiny unit that infects living things and causes disease

novel: new

The coronavirus is surrounded by "spike proteins." This is how the virus attaches to the body.

What Is a Virus?

Viruses are not technically alive. They are not animals or plants. Viruses do not eat, and they do not move on their own. They float in the air or in water. A virus is like a tiny machine. Its job is to make copies of itself.

First, a virus gets inside of a **host**. The mouth and nose are two ways in. Then, the virus slips inside a host's **cell.** Once there, the virus gets to work. It uses parts of the cell to make copies of itself. The copies break out of the cell. Each copy can then spread to a new cell. The copies make even more copies. Soon, the virus is all over. The body becomes sick. It cannot work like normal.

An infected cell will eventually burst, releasing more coronaviruses into the body.

There are many types of viruses. They are a natural part of the world. All plants and animals, including humans, can get viruses. Some viruses make people very sick. Other viruses only cause minor illnesses.

Wearing a mask can protect you and others from getting sick.

CORONAVIRUSES

There are many types of coronavirus. These viruses can only infect certain animals. Birds can catch some coronaviruses. So can mammals, such as dogs and humans.

Seven coronaviruses can make humans sick. Four of them are very common. They cause minor illnesses, like colds. Most people will have a common coronavirus at some point. Three coronaviruses can make people very sick. They can even cause death. SARS-CoV-2 is one of these.

host: the animal or plant in which a virus lives

cell: a very small part of a living being

Not everyone who has COVID-19 has a fever, but it is a common symptom.

Fighting Back

People and animals are not helpless against a virus. The body fights back. Special cells are sent out. They break down the virus.

When the body fights the virus, people feel sick. The body heats up on purpose. This causes a fever. Viruses cannot do their work when it is too hot. People might also have a runny nose. Some get aches and chills. These are signs of the body fighting the virus.

The special cells in the body remember how to beat the virus. If the virus comes back, the person usually has **immunity**. A **vaccine** teaches the body how to fight a virus. With a vaccine, the body has a learned immunity. It does not need to catch the virus first. But with new viruses, no one has immunity yet. Everyone is at risk.

---

immunity: protection from a certain disease

vaccine: a medicine that protects people against a disease

Coronavirus Structure

SPIKES
Spikes are where the virus attaches to a host's cell. The spikes act as keys that open the cell to the virus.

MEMBRANE
A membrane, like a thin outer skin, holds the virus together.

RNA
A piece of RNA is inside the virus. RNA is a set of instructions on how to make copies of the virus.

A Global Pandemic

New viruses are made all the time. In a host, a virus is busy making copies. It uses something called RNA. RNA is a set of instructions. They say how to make the copies. Sometimes mistakes are made. Mistakes can change the RNA. This is called **mutation**. Mutations can make a new virus. Other times, the virus takes **genes** from the host. The virus uses the new genes, and a different virus is made.

SARS-CoV-2 may have started in a bat. Then it mutated. Some scientists think it moved to another animal, such as a pangolin. Pangolins are similar to anteaters. Both animals can carry coronaviruses. From there, the virus may have jumped to a human.

Now, humans can give SARS-CoV-2 to each other. The virus continues to mutate. This makes it hard to track and predict.

DID YOU KNOW?
Scientists think SARS-CoV-2 had mutated at least 30 different times by April 2020.

mutation: a sudden change in biology that causes new or different characteristics

gene: a part of a cell that determines how something develops

Several viruses have passed from bats to humans, including rabies.

Masks, temperature checks, and rules about staying home were common in China during the COVID-19 pandemic.

A Fast-Moving Virus

The first known case of COVID-19 was in late 2019. It was in the city of Wuhan, China. The person may have gotten the virus at an animal market. In late January, the government took action. It shut down Wuhan. But it was too late. People traveled from China to other countries. Visitors returned home. They brought the virus with them. Soon after, Europe and the United States had their first cases.

The virus is very infectious. This means it spreads easily. A person living a normal life can infect two or three people before they have symptoms. The number of sick people grows quickly.

According to the World Health Organization, by February 1, 2020, there were 11,953 **confirmed** cases around the world. On March 1, there were 87,137. By April, the number had grown to 823,626. On May 1, there were 3,175,207 confirmed cases. The virus had spread to nearly every country in the world.

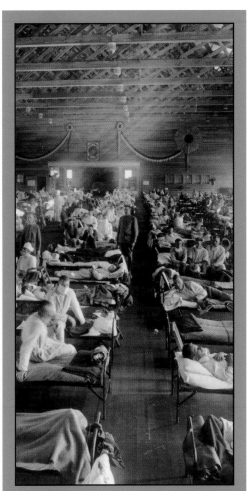

To slow the spread of the virus, many countries banned international travel and required temperature checks and masks before boarding flights.

confirmed: shown to be true

pandemic: a time when a disease spreads quickly over a large area

THE FLU OF 1918

COVID-19 is often compared to another **pandemic**. In 1918, a novel virus emerged. No one had immunity. It spread to all corners of the world. The virus caused the Spanish flu. This flu was very deadly. As many as 50 million people died. At least 550,000 deaths were in the United States.

The top medical research lab in the country is located at Harvard University.

Finding Answers

Researchers want to know how deadly COVID-19 is. If a person gets sick, what is the chance they will recover? What is the chance they will die? This is called the death rate. It is very hard to calculate. Scientists need to know many things. They need to know how many people have the virus. Then they need to know how many of those people eventually died. To get the most accurate results, every single person would be tested. But this is impossible on a large scale.

Instead, scientists use **models**. Models help them make guesses. Early models of COVID-19 were scary. They said the virus could spread quickly. Hospitals would be too crowded. Doctors would not be able to help everyone. The death rate could be 3 or 4 percent. If everyone in a city of 100,000 people caught the virus, 3,000 to 4,000 could die. But if people took action, could that number shrink?

model: a math program that shows future possibilities

COVID-19 Timeline

LATE 2019
The first people become sick in Wuhan, China. Doctors soon identify a novel coronavirus.

JANUARY 2020
The first death from COVID-19 is reported. The virus spreads to many other countries. The United States reports its first cases. They are in Washington state and California.

FEBRUARY 2020
Eight European nations report the disease in early February. Within a month, that grows to 24 nations with 2,200 cases.

MARCH 2020
The World Health Organization declares the outbreak a global pandemic. The United States becomes the new hotspot. All 50 states report cases by March 17. The country reports more than 189,000 cases by the end of the month.

APRIL 2020
The number of cases worldwide begins to lower. Asia and Europe start to open certain businesses back up. The US reports more than 1,000 deaths per day for nearly the entire month. As of April 23, about 26.4 million Americans have filed for unemployment since the beginning of lockdown.

MAY 2020
Leaders from around the world hold a fundraising conference. They pledge $8 billion to scientists working on a vaccine.

Slow the Spread

SARS-CoV-2 spreads through **droplets**. When someone sneezes or coughs, droplets spray into the air. The droplets spread out in a cloud. An uncovered sneeze can travel more than 20 feet (6 meters). A normal breath can move droplets 3 feet (0.9 m). A person might walk through the cloud. Droplets can get into their eyes, nose, or mouth. This person becomes a new host for the virus. This is why health officials say to stay 6 feet (1.8 m) away from others. They also suggest wearing a mask to cover the nose and mouth.

The virus can also stay on surfaces. A sick person might cough onto their hand. Then they touch something, like a doorknob. The virus can stick there for hours or even days. A person might touch the doorknob. Then they rub their nose. The virus gets inside them.

DID YOU KNOW?

SARS-CoV-2 can survive for up to three days on plastic and stainless steel surfaces.

---

droplet: a tiny drop of liquid

The safest way to sneeze is either into a tissue or your elbow crease so the droplets are trapped.

When the Body Reacts

People with COVID-19 do not feel sick right away. The virus needs time to build up new copies. It grows in the throat and lungs. Then **symptoms** begin. This usually takes five days. Sometimes, it takes up to two weeks.

Most people recover. Their body fights off the virus. They feel sick for a week or two. Then they get better. Other people might have a weakened **immune system**. They might be elderly or already sick. Their bodies cannot fight the virus very well. The death rate is between 10 and 27 percent for elderly people.

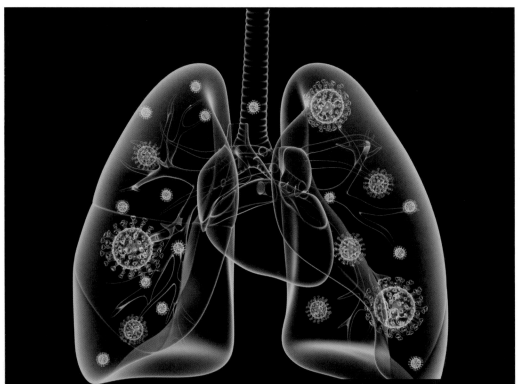

Lungs are like spongy balloons. They expand with air when we breathe. COVID-19 can damage the lungs.

In some cases, the immune system overreacts. Doctors do not understand why. This creates a lot of fluid. The fluid builds up in the lungs. Breathing becomes hard. People need machines to help them breathe. These machines are called ventilators. If the immune system cannot beat the virus, COVID-19 continues to spread through the body. Eventually, the person dies.

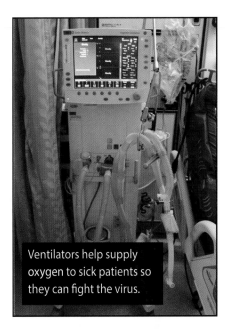

Ventilators help supply oxygen to sick patients so they can fight the virus.

SYMPTOMS OF COVID-19

For most people, COVID-19 feels like a regular flu or cold. They have a fever and feel tired and achy. They might have a sore throat. A dry cough is also common. These people usually get better on their own. People who have trouble breathing should call their doctor. They might not get enough air. Their lips or face might turn blue. Confusion or grogginess might occur. These people need help right away.

symptom: a change in the body that is a sign of sickness

immune system: the organs, tissues, and cells in the body that fight sickness

Protect Yourself

Health officials are asking people to make safe choices. They know the best way to slow the spread is through **isolation** and social distancing. The virus cannot pass from person to person if everyone stays home. People who are sick, elderly, or have weakened immune systems should stay home. Others should stay home as much as they can. These measures keep the number of COVID-19 cases down and make sure hospitals can help people that are ill.

isolation: the state of staying separate from others

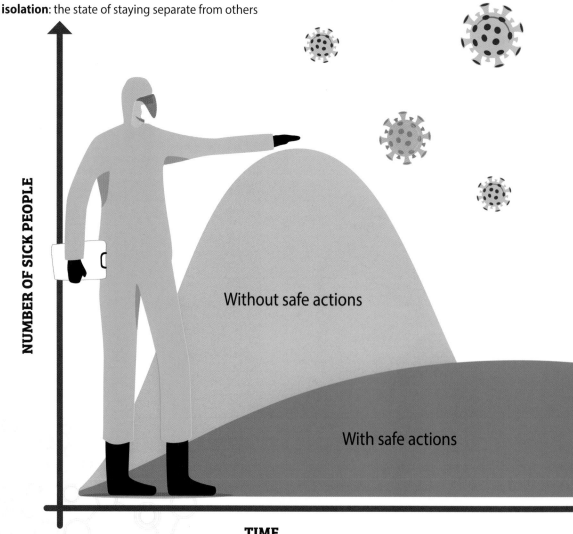

NUMBER OF SICK PEOPLE

Without safe actions

With safe actions

TIME

When washing hands, make sure to scrub the palm, the thumbs, between the fingers, and around the nails.

In public, wear a cloth mask. Keep a safe distance from others. Staying 6 feet (1.8 m) apart keeps you out of other people's air droplet clouds. Don't touch your eyes, nose, or mouth. Wash your hands often. Soap is made up of many tiny parts. These tiny parts surround the coronavirus. They break into its membrane. Then they tear the virus apart. The soap traps the parts of the virus. Everything is rinsed down the drain.

What Happens Next

There is only one way for a pandemic to end. The majority of people need to have immunity. Those people do not spread the virus. Then the virus will die out. This is called herd immunity.

There are two ways to reach herd immunity. The safest way is through a vaccine. The other may be through natural immunity. For natural immunity to work, people must catch COVID-19. Their special cells learn how to fight the virus. Then their bodies are protected. The United States has been working toward widespread testing. It is the only way to know how many people have had COVID-19.

Experts think at least 70 percent of people need immunity from a virus to make a difference. In the United States, that's about 231 million people. Everyone does not need to get sick at once for herd immunity to work. Hospitals would be overrun. That is why people try to slow the spread. Doctors can then help everyone.

DID YOU KNOW?

As of April 2020, researchers were exploring more than 60 different vaccines for COVID-19.

Tests are a very important way doctors and scientists can track and understand this new virus.

What About a Vaccine?

The second path to herd immunity is a vaccine. A vaccine would bring immunity to most people. This way, fewer people would have to catch the virus.

Unfortunately, vaccines take many years to create. First, scientists need to do research. They pick out a type of vaccine to try. Then they test it. Testing takes a long time.

A vaccine must be safe. It cannot have dangerous **side effects**. The vaccine must also work. It has to be good at creating immunity. Human testing often lasts for months or even years. This makes sure a vaccine both works and is safe for humans. Once a vaccine is created, it is **manufactured**. Hundreds of millions of doses are needed.

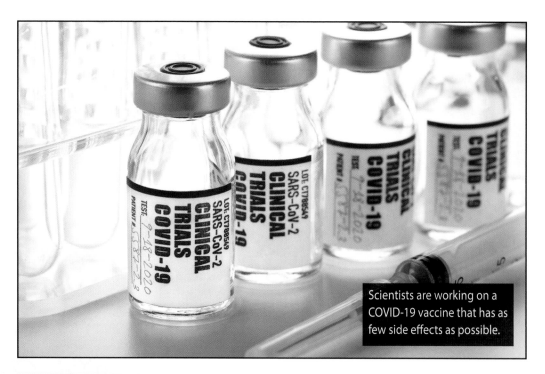

Scientists are working on a COVID-19 vaccine that has as few side effects as possible.

side effect: an unwanted or harmful result from taking medicine

manufacture: to make, usually by large amounts in a factory

Scientists are exploring new types of vaccines to treat COVID-19. Since it is so widespread, they are trying to speed up the process. They hope to have a vaccine by mid-2021. Scientists are also trying many different treatments. They may not cure the virus, but they could help people recover faster.

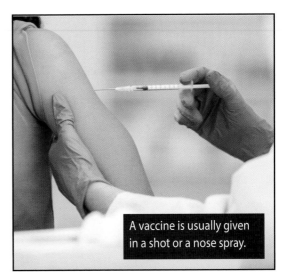

A vaccine is usually given in a shot or a nose spray.

DID YOU KNOW?
The fastest vaccine ever created was for the mumps. It took four years in the 1960s.

MEDICINE FOR COVID-10

Experts are hard at work on medicine for COVID-19. Medicine can help with symptoms. It can keep some people from dying. One option is **antiviral** medicines. Many antiviral medicines already exist. Researchers are seeing if they work for COVID-19.

Other medicines use **antibodies**. Antibodies block a virus from host cells. This type of medicine is used to treat cancer. Now doctors want to use it for possible COVID-19 treatments.

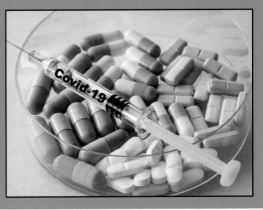

antiviral: able to destroy a virus

antibody: a unit in the body that attaches to and stops a virus

A Global Response

Countries have been taking different actions. In the United States, schools and businesses closed quickly. By the end of April, there were 168 deaths for every 1 million people.

Sweden took a different approach. Leaders chose to keep the **economy** open. Grade schools, restaurants, and many businesses stayed open. People were encouraged to work from home. By the end of April, Sweden had 220 deaths for every 1 million people. But models said the country had close to 25% immunity. They guessed herd immunity would be reached in May.

There is no quick fix for a pandemic. Herd immunity or a vaccine might take years. Experts are trying to find a balance. They want to keep people safe and also keep economies going.

economy: a country's system of producing, buying, and selling goods and services

Using hand sanitizer is a quick way to disinfect when soap and water aren't available.

US Testing for COVID-19

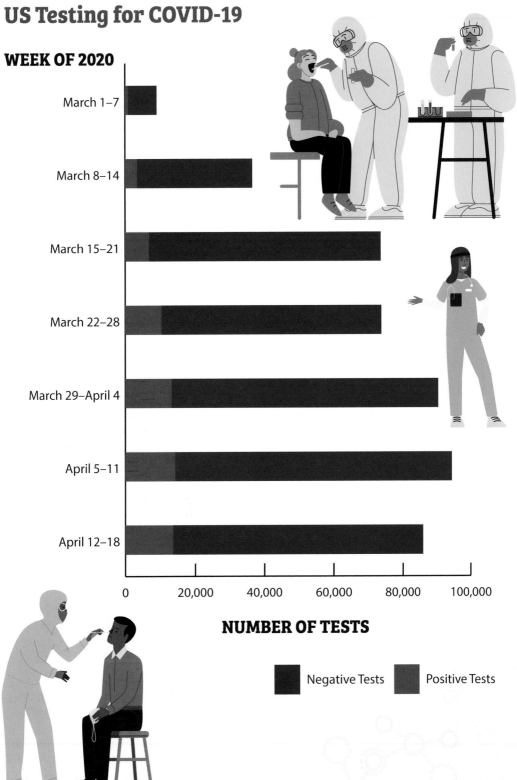

WEEK OF 2020

	NUMBER OF TESTS
March 1–7	
March 8–14	
March 15–21	
March 22–28	
March 29–April 4	
April 5–11	
April 12–18	

0   20,000   40,000   60,000   80,000   100,000

NUMBER OF TESTS

■ Negative Tests   ■ Positive Tests

QUIZ

1. What is a virus's main job?

2. What is inside a coronavirus?

3. How can a new virus be made?

4. When was the COVID-19 outbreak declared a global pandemic?

5. How does SARS-CoV-2 spread?

6. How long does it usually take for symptoms to begin?

7. What is the best way to slow the spread?

8. What are the two ways to herd immunity?

8. Natural immunity and a vaccine
7. Isolation
6. Five days
5. Through air droplets
4. March 2020
3. Mutation or taking genes from the host
2. A piece of RNA
1. To make copies of itself.

RESEARCH A VIRUS

Viruses are constantly mutating and changing. New viruses are created. This is your chance to find out more about a virus. Share what you learn with your family and classmates.

MATERIALS

- Internet access
- Pencil and paper
- Construction paper
- Scissors
- Glue

STEPS

1. Research the different types of viruses. How are they different from coronaviruses? How are they similar?

2. Pick a virus that you want to learn more about. What does it look like? How does it enter a host? Draw a sketch of the virus. Label the parts.

3. Use construction paper to make a picture of the virus. Use a different color to cut out each part. Glue all the pieces together.

4. Show the virus to your family, friends, and classmates. Explain what each part of the virus does.

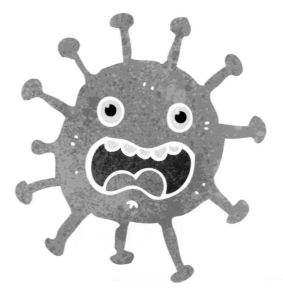

GLOSSARY

antibody: a unit in the body that attaches to and stops a virus

antiviral: able to destroy a virus

cell: a very small part of a living being

confirmed: shown to be true

droplet: a tiny drop of liquid

economy: a country's system of producing, buying, and selling goods and services

gene: a part of a cell that determines how something develops

host: the animal or plant in which a virus lives

immune system: the organs, tissues, and cells in the body that fight sickness

immunity: protection from a certain disease

isolation: the state of staying separate from others

manufacture: to make, usually by large amounts in a factory

model: a math program that shows future possibilities

mutation: a sudden change in biology that causes new or different characteristics

novel: new

pandemic: a time when a disease spreads quickly over a large area

side effect: an unwanted or harmful result from taking medicine

symptom: a change in the body that is a sign of sickness

vaccine: a medicine that protects people against a disease

virus: a tiny unit that infects living things and causes disease

READ MORE

Cline-Ransome, Lesa. *Germs: Fact and Fiction, Friends and Foes.* New York: Henry Holt and Company, 2017.

Koontz, Robin Michal. *The Science of a Pandemic.* Disaster Science. Ann Arbor, MI: Cherry Lake, 2015.

Marciniak, Kristin. *Flu Pandemic of 1918.* History's Greatest Disasters. Minneapolis: ABDO, 2014.

Morey, Allan. *Global Pandemic.* It's the End of the World. Minneapolis: Bellwether Media, Inc., 2020.

Rogers, Kara. *Engineering Solutions for Epidemics and Pandemics.* Preparing for Disaster. New York: Rosen, 2020.

INTERNET SITES

https://www.livescience.com/coronavirus-kids-guide.html
Live Science explains the coronavirus for kids.

https://youtu.be/R-JbDMYmAQM
Watch a video on the coronavirus with Dr. Bioncs.

https://kidshealth.org/en/kids/coronavirus-kids.html?WT.ac=p-ra
Learn what you can do to prevent COVID-19.

https://www.cdc.gov/mobile/applications/sto/web-app.html
Play a game to learn about investigating and solving virus outbreaks.

https://kids.nationalgeographic.com/explore/science/facts-about-coronavirus
Read more about the coronavirus with National Geographic Kids.

INDEX